Face to Face

Helping someone grow,
one to one

Face to Face

Printed by Printed
www.printed.com
Printed in Great Britain

Contents

A great idea

Maturing and developing as a follower of Jesus is not automatic. It takes time and we all need help to 'grow up in every way into him who is the head, into Christ' (Ephesians 4:15).

This booklet will help you think about how you might get alongside one other person, meeting with them one to one and helping them to 'live a life worthy of the Lord and please him in every way' (Colossians 1:10 NIV).

Jesus did it. He walked alongside 12 individuals, teaching them how to live life with him and how to live life like him. He also wants us to 'walk in the same way in which he walked' (1 John 2:6).

Just as Jesus commissioned his first disciples, he wants us to do the same, to 'go therefore and make disciples of all nations' (Matthew 28:19). Jesus wants us to teach others what it looks like to follow him with the whole of their lives, for the whole of their lives.

Face to Face sets out a framework, but do not feel confined by it. Meeting one to one with another person is founded on a living relationship with Jesus, which means it is dynamic, not 'one size fits all'. Let Jesus guide you by his Spirit.

What does it look like?

Tamsin's story

'Before I went to university, no one had ever met with me one to one and helped me grow. I knew Jesus and I wanted to live my life for him but I didn't know how to. At university that all changed. For two years on a regular basis, someone met with me one to one. She provided a space where I could be myself, where I could share, ask, discover and grow. She helped me understand more about the life Jesus wants me to live and shared her own walk with Jesus with me. She also reflected the love and grace of God to me. Having that space, care and help resulted in significant growth. It transformed me.'

It is one person helping another grow in their relationship with God. You may not consider yourself to be a leader or a mature Christian, but God has given you all you need to help someone take their next step.

How does it work?

- **It is God** at work by his Spirit (John 14:16-17). He will help and equip you as you get alongside someone. He will also deepen the other person's understanding, love and trust of him. He will bring transformation to you both, and you can be 'sure of this, that he who began a good work in you [both] will bring it to completion' (Philippians 1:6).

- **It is you** deepening your friendship with Jesus, so that you can say, 'Follow my example, as I follow the example of Christ' (1 Corinthians 11:1 NIV). It is you also helping them discover how to 'walk in a manner worthy of the calling to which you have been called' that they too may 'be filled with all the fullness of God' (Ephesians 4:1, 3:19).

- **It is the other person** seeking to grow, to be 'rooted and built up in him and established in the faith' (Colossians 2:7). It is the other person also becoming someone who desires to share Jesus with those that don't know him yet and help those that know him to grow. Then they too can live out the Great Commission (Matthew 28:18-20).

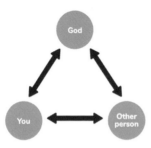

Top tip

Consider asking a more mature Christian to meet up with you one to one, to encourage you in your walk with Jesus as you help someone else.

'Where are we going in disciple-making? What is the goal? Maturity. A mature person is equipped to serve, someone who knows God and his Word and someone with Christ-like character.'

Dirk van Zuylen
past National Director, Navigators UK

How
to
get
ready

A one-to-one is not primarily about us and our contribution or even about the person we are helping and their progress. One-to-ones are about developing a relationship with Jesus and fully submitting our lives to him. So we prepare by focusing our heart on Jesus.

Getting ready to ask someone

- **Ask Jesus** to guide you and to help you know who to meet with.

- **Don't ask just anyone**. Ask someone who is seeking to grow.

- **Don't ask everyone**. Start with one person and go from there. If you meet with too many people you won't have the time or resources to be able to invest in them.

> **Top tip**
>
> Don't just ask people you naturally get on with or who are like you. Ask the people the Lord lays on your heart.

'Where's your man? Where's your woman? Where's that one for whom you are pouring out your life to help them walk with Christ?'

Dawson Trotman
founder of The Navigators

Getting yourself ready

Prayerfully
Depending on God in prayer is the foundation for meeting one to one with someone. Just like Jesus, we need God's help (John 8:28, John 15:5), so spend time with him, speaking, waiting and listening. Be energised and empowered by his Spirit. 'Look to the Lord and his strength; seek his face always' (1 Chronicles 16:11 NIV).

Personally
Jesus shared his whole life with his disciples – his sufferings, strengths, joys and sorrows. Paul did this too: 'We loved you so much, we were delighted to share with you not only the gospel of God but our lives as well' (1 Thessalonians 2:8 NIV). Sharing your whole life, including the mundane bits, requires wise vulnerability. It may be awkward and uncomfortable at times, but if you want to help someone walk with Jesus every day, they need to see you do that.

Purposefully
Create a plan before you meet with someone. There is an old saying, 'Most people aim at nothing and hit it with amazing accuracy', so put thought into your one-to-one. Think about where this person is on their journey with Jesus (see below) and how you might best serve them. As you depend on God, ask him to give you direction. God knows this person intimately and is the greatest authority on them (Psalm 139:1).

Where are they on their journey?

- Evangelism – If they aren't a Christian, help them encounter Jesus and see what he is like, to become a believer

- Establishing – If they are a young Christian, help them to follow Jesus day by day, to know him better and to understand what life with him looks like, to become a disciple

- Equipping – If they are already established, help them to grow in love and to get alongside others to share Jesus, to become a labourer

- Sending – If they are already helping others to grow, help them teach those people how to get alongside others, all the while going deeper with God, as they go out into the harvest field

Ideas for resources for each stage are given at the end of the booklet.

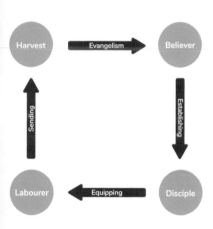

Getting ready to meet

Plan a regular time and day, weekly or fortnightly

Find a place where you can easily talk, read and pray together

- During each meeting, always make arrangements for next time

- Keep in touch in between meetings

- Expect God to work

Top tip

Mix it up with less formal meetings such as meals, walks, sports or games, especially at the beginning as you develop your friendship and trust.

Sakura's story

'Throughout my time at university I regularly met with someone one to one. This had a significant impact in my walk with the Lord. When I started leading a small group I was excited to meet one to one with some of the girls in the group because I personally had found it so helpful. Although I had experienced one-to-ones, I found it hard to know where to begin and who to ask. I felt inadequate and worried about my ability to ask good questions that would lead to 'super spiritual' conversations. These insecurities held me back. However, I was reminded that my worth is not in how well I ask questions, if I choose the perfect book to read together, or how spiritual our conversations will be. I learned to trust God to use me and the time I spent with them. As I learned to listen to God and the person in front of me, I began to see how the Holy Spirit was working in their lives. It was a privilege to see God at work in this way.'

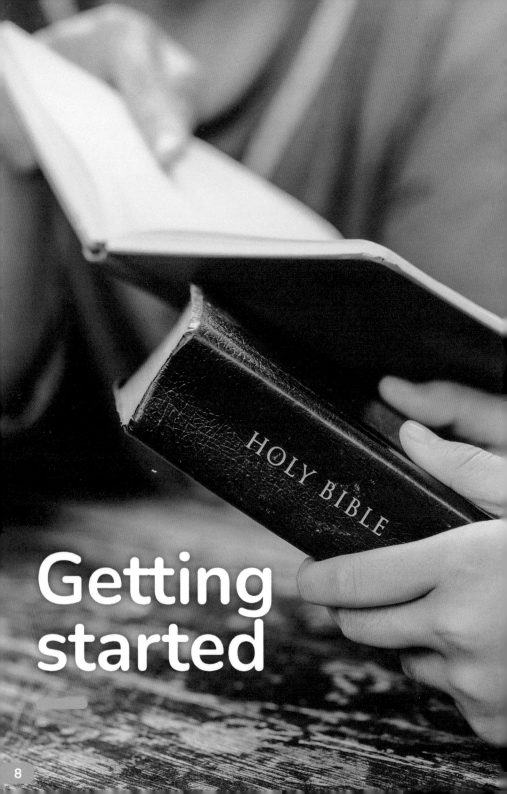

Getting started

Form a friendship

Before diving into the deep end, it is good to spend time getting to know each other. This fosters trust and enables you to better serve them. Do something fun together, ask about their passions in life and their background, invite them to share about how they came to follow Jesus and share your story with them. (Safeguarding guidelines are given at the end of the booklet.)

Top tip

For some people, often males, a coffee shop is not the optimal environment for meeting one to one. Doing life shoulder to shoulder rather than face to face might be more beneficial, such as going for a walk, playing sport or watching a film.

Although talking to and about God is essential, we must be careful not to create a sacred-secular divide. God is interested in all areas of our lives and is Lord over every part. After all, 'In him we live and move and have our being' (Acts 17:28). It is normal and natural to talk about other things.

Ask questions about:

- Their morning/day/week

- Their hobbies, job, social life, sports, etc.

- Things you have previously talked about, such as important events

Ask open questions

This skill takes a lifetime to learn, but be assured the Holy Spirit will lead and guide you. A good question fosters understanding, brings things into the light and gives direction. It helps the person you're meeting with dive deeper. The best questions are open not closed, inviting conversation.

Helpful questions

- What do you sense God might be saying or doing in this situation? (This takes the focus off you and your ideas and puts it rightfully on God and his wisdom.)

- How are you finding loving God at the moment? How are you experiencing his love?

- How are you finding spending time with God?

- What is distancing you from Jesus? What is helping you draw near to Jesus?

- How are you seeking to share Jesus with others?

- How are your relationships with others?

Listen well

Always 'be quick to hear, slow to speak' (James 1:19). Why? Because 'the purposes of a person's heart are deep waters, but one who has insight draws them out' (Proverbs 20:5 NIV). When we listen, we create space that the other person can fill and, with the help of the Holy Spirit, we can discover what is in the depths of their heart.

Ways to listen

- Show you're listening by your body language, eye contact and affirming noises (umms and arrhs).

- Embrace silence – God is at work in it.

- Reflect back to them what they have said and clarify what they mean.

- Listen with humility – don't try to fix them.

- Put your phone away and on silent.

- Be present and trust the Holy Spirit to guide the conversation and give you the words to say.

- If possible, meet in person rather than online to connect more fully.

Ways we 'listen' that aren't really listening

- Pretend listening – you look like you are listening but you aren't actually taking anything in.

- Playback listening – you are able to repeat back to them what they have said but you haven't taken it in.

- Part listening – your own thoughts intermingle with what's being said so you only partly hear them.

- Predictive listening – you stop listening in order to think about what you might say or panic about not knowing what to say.

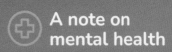

A note on mental health

We want open and honest conversation. If they share about struggles that you aren't qualified to help with, don't panic. Refer them to a GP, counsellor, etc. Continue to walk beside them if you feel able, but remember that it is not your job to fix them.

Consider God's Word

Whilst good listening, insights and questions are helpful, the real power behind a one-to-one lies in engaging with God's Word. For 'the word of God is living and active, sharper than any two-edged sword' (Hebrews 4:12). It brings transformation.

Ways to look at God's Word together:

Study a book of the Bible
Start with one of the Gospels or one of Paul's letters. Ask questions like

- *What does it say?* Read, underline, annotate, note down questions.

- *What does it mean?* Use context, cross references, a dictionary or a commentary to answer your questions and discern the passage's meaning.

- *What difference does it make?* What might God be saying to you both through the passage? Consider what you might do as a result.

Work through a topical Bible study

Choose a relevant topic. Look up places in the Bible that refer to the topic and words associated with it (websites like Biblehub, Biblegateway and STEP Bible are helpful).

Make notes on what the Bible says about the topic.

Summarise what you have discovered.

Pray about how God wants to use this in each of your lives.

Do a Bible read through

You could use a Bible reading plan and read some sections aloud together and some separately, discussing as you go.

Memorise and meditate on verses

Learn to hide God's Word in your hearts by helping each other learn and practise Bible verses.

Look at a Christian book together

Although these don't have the same authority as the Bible, there are many biblically based books that are helpful.

'I am here at your side, let's talk this over, let's consider how we can get in on everything God is doing.'

Eugene Peterson
author of *The Message*

Engage in prayer

Pray before your one-to-one, during and after. Beforehand, entrust into God's care both you and the person you are helping. Ask the Holy Spirit to be at work. During, pray over issues that arise. Paul told some young Christians to 'pray in the Spirit on all occasions with all kinds of prayers and requests' (Ephesians 6:18 NIV). Demonstrate that God cares about the big things in the whole world, but also about the details of your life.

Praying out loud takes practice. You might feel awkward at first, but don't give up. It is a new and important habit to learn as you lead your one-to-ones. But you may want to hold off praying out loud in your first few meetings as you grow comfortable with the person you are helping.

Don't wait too long to encourage them to pray as well. Set a pattern where both of you pray, because it's important for them to personally engage with God. Pray for them and their needs, and then encourage them to pray for you, following your example. This gives you an opportunity to be vulnerable. Paul told the young Christians in his life, 'Pray also for me...' (Ephesians 6:19 NIV). No matter how long you have walked with Jesus, you always need prayer.

What is prayer? It is simply communicating with God.

> 'Prayer is Christ's invitation to an intoxicating relationship in his promises, presence and power. It is a gift that keeps us walking on water with Christ in all life's storms. It is an exciting opportunity to join Christ on a faith adventure in everyday life.'
>
> **Bernard Dishman**
> Navigators UK

And when we share this kind of an adventure within our one-to-ones, we open the door for God to work deeply.

Top tip

After your one-to-one, make notes on how it went, things you might want to remember they said, prayer points. Think ahead to next time, about what you might want to do as a result? Be careful to keep such notes private as some of the information may be sensitive.

Ben's story

'Everyone is different. Some people love coffee shops, others love adventure. Some like to meet at the same time and place every week, while for others the relationship does not feel genuine unless it's slightly unplanned. During some one-to-ones, I always read the Bible, and in others it was not always planned and rarely happened. I once met with someone and we didn't really have anything to say. I suggested we pray and he agreed, so we prayed and carried on with our day. I consider that meeting memorable and valuable – despite not knowing what was achieved. In love, we can consider the best environment for the type of person and type of chat, but we can't always choose when 'break through' moments might come. I want to carry the same expectation that God will be at work in both the mundane and set apart meetings. I never quite know what will happen, but I do know that if I set the time aside and bring it before God, that he is with us, and at work in us by his Holy Spirit – whether watching football, walking on the beach, serving together, or sitting face to face down the pub with our Bibles open.'

In a
nutshell

Focus your heart on Jesus

 Ask someone

 Create a plan

 Expect God to work

 Form a friendship

 Ask questions and listen well

 Consider God's Word

 Engage in prayer

Pass
it on

You are limited in how many people you are able to meet up with one to one. In order for the Great Commission to be fulfilled, the buck can't stop with you. An essential part of meeting one to one is encouraging and helping the person you meet with to do the same with others. When Paul walked alongside Timothy, he encouraged him to walk alongside others, who would in turn do the same. He said, 'the things you have heard me say in the presence of many witnesses entrust to reliable people who will also be qualified to teach others' (2 Timothy 2:2 NIV).

Here is a simple way to pass it on

- **Tell them why**
  Explain to them why one-to-ones are a great idea: to enable someone to live the life Jesus has for them. Share stories of how different one-to-one friendships have shaped you.

- **Show them how**
  Much of what someone learns from you comes from observing and imitating what you do. Make it easy for them to copy you by doing things with them, such as spending time with God together, doing Bible study, memorising Bible verses, and praying. Let them see how you share your story and listen well.

- **Get them started**
  Give them this booklet. Help them think through who to ask, how to ask and what they might do with that person. Pray about it with them.

- **Keep them going**
  Provide them with space to process how their one-to-one is going. Pass on helpful resources and pray with them about it.

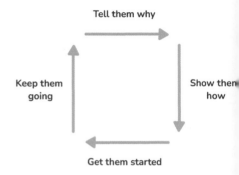

'It may be slow, building into a few lives at a time, and it may take years to see them become well established in life and service, but it works. That is the wonder of generations: they reproduce.'

Brian Blacklock
author of *Pass the Baton*

Meeting one to one is a privilege that God has entrusted to us, out of his immense love. He helps us along the way and enables us, for he 'is able to do immeasurably more than all we ask or imagine, according to his power that is at work within us' (Ephesians 3:20 NIV). His Holy Spirit is with us.

Safeguarding guidelines

Sometimes the people we meet up with are vulnerable and we might not know it. Care needs to be taken to protect them and you.

Here are some helpful boundaries

Meet in a public place, not behind closed doors.

Do not have any physical contact, other than what is initiated by the other person, is honourable and you are comfortable with.

Don't record your times together or put photos up on social media, except with prior permission.

Don't spend excessive amounts of time together.

Enjoy your times together, but stay safe and be smart.

The author

Shona Cullens helps lead the Navigator student ministry in Stirling, Scotland, and has helped many people grow through one-to-ones. She is a musician and she and her husband Duncan compose and sing original worship songs. She also enjoys long walks with her dog Barney.

Contributors

Shona wrote this booklet using materials developed by a range of Navigator one-to-one leaders as inspiration. Contributions came from Navigator Reps and Associates across the UK with a variety of ministry expertise, including Darren Jackson (counsellor and ministry leader), Ros Boydell (Scottish ministry leader), Bernard Dishman, Colin Gillies and Tim Yearsley (student ministry leaders), Mike Spencer (young adult ministry leader), Ted Pilling (Second Half Living outreach), Mike and Chris Treneer (international leader training) and Derek Leaf (Country Leader, Navigators UK).

Other Resources

Navigators UK produce a number of resources that might be helpful for you in your one-to-ones. Different resources are appropriate for different discipleship stages. All are available from:

navigators.co.uk/online-shop

Discover Jesus

A Bible study that helps someone investigate the Christian message for the firs time.

Price: £4.00
Paperback: 44 pages

Establishing

First Encounters

A series of Bible studies that cover the basics someone needs to know when they become a Christian.

Price: £4.00
Paperback: 44 pages

Establishing

Time Out With God

A step-by-step guide to gettir to know God by making a hat of spending time with him ea day.

Price: £2.50
Paperback: 20 pages

Establishing

Life Series

Bible studies on life issues of work, sex and mental wellbeing.

Price: £4.00 each

Equipping

The Art of Leading a Smal Group

A practical guidebook for small-group leaders, whethe you're starting out, already established or handing over.

Price: £2.50
Paperback: 20 pages

Equipping

Living the Conversation

A practical guide for anyone who wants to share Jesus but struggles to bring him into conversations.

Price: £2.50
Paperback: 24 pages

Sending

Pass the Baton

A book that shows someone how to run alongside others to pass on what God has given them.

Price: £4.50
Paperback: 70 pages